Those who use ritual magic in their daily lives have grown disenchanted with the sterility of modern Western society. They seek fulfillment and purpose, and they have found that ritual magic is a viable means for change—not only on the physical but on the emotional and mental levels as well.

Now you can learn what magicians already know—that using your inborn magical ability is simply a matter of knowledge and practice. *The Truth About Ritual Magic* explains the concepts and intent underlying the practice of ritual magic in clear, easily understandable terms.

Learn why practicing ritual magic can free you from the prison of the present and allow you to more consciously shape your life … discover why the barrier that divides you from the world around you is an illusion … and experience how performing ritual magic can beneficially change your view of yourself and the world around you.

About the Author

Donald Tyson is a Canadian from Halifax, Nova Scotia. He devotes his life to the attainment of a complete gnosis of the art of magic in theory and practice. His purpose is to formulate an accessible system of personal training composed of East and West, past and present, that will help the individual discover the reason for one's existence and a way to fulfill it.

To Write to the Author

If you wish to contact the author or would like more information about this book, please write to the author in care of Llewellyn Worldwide and we will forward your request. Both the author and publisher appreciate hearing from you and learning of your enjoyment of this book and how it has helped you. Llewellyn Worldwide cannot guarantee that every letter written to the author can be answered, but all will be forwarded. Please write to:

Donald Tyson
c/o Llewellyn Worldwide
P.O. Box 64383-830, St. Paul, MN 55164-0383, U.S.A.

Please enclose a self-addressed, stamped envelope for reply, or $1.00 to cover costs.
If outside U.S.A., enclose International postal reply coupon.

Free Catalog From Llewellyn

For more than 90 years Llewellyn has brought its readers knowledge in the fields of metaphysics and human potential. Learn about the newest books in spiritual guidance, natural healing, astrology, occult philosophy, and more. Enjoy book reviews, new age articles, a calender of events, plus current products and services. To get your free copy of *Llewellyn's New Worlds of Mind and Spirit,* send your name and address to:

Llewellyn's New Worlds of Mind and Spirit
P.O. Box 64383-830, St. Paul, MN 55164-0383, U.S.A.

LLEWELLYN'S VANGUARD SERIES

The Truth About

RITUAL MAGIC

by Donald Tyson

1994
Llewellyn Publications
St. Paul, MN 55164-0383, U.S.A.

FIRST EDITION, 1989
Second Edition
First Printing, 1994

International Standard Book Number:
0-87542-830-4

Cover illustration by James & Anne Marie Garrison

LLEWELLYN PUBLICATIONS
A Division of Llewellyn Worldwide, Ltd.
P.O. Box 64383, St. Paul, MN 55164-0383

Other Books by Donald Tyson

The New Magus, 1988
Rune Magic, 1988
The Truth About Runes, 1989
How to Make and Use a Magic Mirror, 1990
Ritual Magic, 1991
The Messenger, 1993

Cards and Kits by Donald Tyson

Rune Magic Deck, 1988
Power of the Runes, 1989

Editor and Annotator

Three Books of Occult Philosophy by
Henry Cornelius Agrippa
Von Hettesheim, 1993

Forthcoming:

Tetragrammaton: The Wonder-Working Name

MAGIC IS ALIVE

Magic is real. It exists. It works. It is the most potent and beautiful force in the universe. Magic is the flowing lifeblood of the Soul of the World. It is the essence that separates the living from the dead. It is the divine gift that renders humankind immortal.

There is nothing more important or more necessary than magic. And it is everywhere. In the waves of the sea and the twinkle of a star; in the sap of a leaf and the sweetness of a nut, in the sigh of the wind and the song of a bird. The world is a living thing, and magic is its beating heart.

To know magic you must be willing to accept that there is more to your life than eating, sleeping, copulating and dying. Magic moves below the surface of things. It can give you inner peace and self-confidence, personal magnetism, the power to attain your goals in life, and most important of all, a true understanding of yourself and your place in the universe.

WHAT IS MAGIC?

Magic is an art. In common with other arts, it draws its power from a deep well in the center of the human soul. Within this well are the waters of the unconscious, and below the surface dwell all possibilities and potentials, awaiting their turn to be pulled up into the light and made real. So long as they remain under the surface, they do not exist, but the moment they are captured and brought forth they come to be.

This act of pulling a possibility from the well of potential into being is an act of creation. Every creative act is magical. And every magical act is creative. The difference between magic and painting is that the painter creates the canvas, while the canvas of the Magus is the world.

In *The New Magus* I define magic as the art of affecting the manifest through the Unmanifest. The manifest is all that can be seen, touched, perceived, manipulated, imagined, or understood. The Unmanifest is none of these things. It is the place, or rather the non-place, from which everything issues. All that comes into being comes from the Unmanifest. All that passes away goes back to the Unmanifest. This includes each human soul. This passage between manifest and Unmanifest, which I call the Veil of Unknowing, is completed by ideal forms, not material substances. The soul comes into being and passes away—the body is built from clay, and to clay it returns.

It follows that every magical act is a communion with God, however the deity may be conceived or defined by the individual. In fact it is not necessary to talk about God in connection with magic, which is a technique for causing real change in the world that has little to do with common religious sensibility. But it must be stated that magic taps this ultimate source of creation and power. Magic has been trivialized precisely because this fundamental connection has not been grasped.

Many common events that are not considered to be occult are magical. All artistic creation, for example, draws upon the hidden well of potential. Even more everyday occurrences, such as the sudden unexpected awareness of the beauty of a sunrise, or a completely unpremeditated, generous, and loving action, or the sense of absolute inner peace and rightness, are magical happenings in the true sense.

Once the nature of magic is understood, several important insights follow. Since magic reaches beyond the limits of the natural world, it transcends cause and effect. For this reason, magic cannot be predicted with certainty. The same magical ritual does not always produce the same result, or a result at the same time and place. The uncertainty of magic makes it impossible to verify by the scientific method. Attempts to pin down magic with experiments and machines are doomed from the start. What can be predicted is not magic—what is magic cannot be predicted.

One of the corollaries to my definition of magic is that magic in action looks like luck. Those who practice ritual know that it works, but cannot always say where or in what manner the working will take effect. This is very frustrating to scientists, who are inclined to dismiss the entire subject. The psychiatrist Carl Jung came close to understanding the mechanism of magic with his examination of the phenomenon of synchronicity—the seemingly chance co-occurrence of significantly related events. Such fortuitous coincidences, for better or for worse, indicate the working of magic, which is usually unconscious on the part of the worker.

Magic, like water, always seeks the easiest course to the sea. It is seldom spectacular because it seldom needs to be. Once a desire has been formulated, and a ritual conducted to bring it about, magic acts in the simplest and most mundane way to allow the fulfillment of that desire. The Magus must then follow up the possibility for fulfillment that magic has opened, or it will be lost. If you desire to eat an apple, magic can put the apple into your hand, but you have to bite it yourself. If there is an obstacle in your way, one that you cannot physically surmount, magic will make it possible for you to bypass that barrier in some manner or other, even if the obstacle seems impassable. If spectacular results are absolutely necessary, magic is spectacular.

Another interesting aspect of magic is that it is unbounded by time. A magical effect can actually take place before you work the ritual; nonetheless the working of the ritual is a necessary part of the fulfillment of the ritual desire. The late Aleister Crowley noticed this curious effect, and commented upon it:

> "I have noticed that the effect of a Magical Work has followed it so closely that it must have been started before the time of the Work. E. g., I work tonight to make X in Paris write to me. I get the letter the next morning, so that it must have been written before the Work. Does this deny the Work caused the effect?"
>
> —*Magick in Theory and Practice*
> Chapter IX, Dover, New York, 1976,
> pp. 74-5.

It may sound fantastic to those who have not personally experienced the effects of magic, but after occult meditations, I occasionally have found myself thinking forward in time. An idea will come into my mind, often a new and subtle philosophical concept, and I will have no notion what can have sparked it; then a few days later I will be reading, and there is the idea, which I had several days before plucked out of the future of my mindstream. This serves to emphasize the unpredictability of magic while underlining its astounding potential.

It is not necessary to know how magic works in order to work magic. In diverse cultures around the world, magic is practiced by simple people who are not philosophical in the least. They use magic to help them overcome the practical everyday problems that arise in their lives, or to help others around them solve similar problems. Magic is an art that can be employed for both exalted and crass purposes. To use magic to charm away warts, for example, is like playing "Chopsticks" on a Steinway concert grand piano. But the warts will vanish. The work that is done within any art depends on the ability and intention of the artist.

WHAT IS RITUAL?

Ritual is the medium through which the art of magic is practiced. It consists of an action or series of actions, which may be entirely mental, or mental and physical, by which the power of magic is released and directed towards the fulfillment of a specific desire.

Magic ritual is not some strange, exotic beast difficult to approach and apt to scamper away when touched. It is a common occurrence in everyday life. The reason most everyday rituals do not bring about desired effects is that they are not understood for what they truly are; therefore, they remain unfocused.

When a ritual is unfocused, it can never accomplish a major purpose. The magnitude of a ritual is determined by the degree to which the power released is effective power. If power is released in all directions, so to speak, it accomplishes nothing, and the ritual is impotent. Once you become aware that you are working a ritual, and what the purpose of that ritual is, it becomes effective, and magical power is released and applied to the object of desire.

It is doubtful if magic can be worked without ritual. Often the ritual is very brief and completely mental—the inner utterance of a single word, for example. But for the power of magic to be released and directed requires some structure or framework, however simple. To work magic without ritual would be like trying to draw water out of a well without a bucket. Ritual is the bucket. The water itself is the magical potency. The act of drawing it forth is the practice of the art of magic. It can then be carried in the bucket to the place where it will be used, and this is the focusing of the ritual upon the object of desire.

WHAT YOU CAN EXPECT FROM RITUAL MAGIC

Those who approach ritual magic for the first time usually harbor wildly unrealistic expectations shaped by their confused and erroneous notions of what magic is and how it works. There is nothing wrong with this—the practice of magic is a learning process. We learn by doing, and making mistakes. Here I would like to give some idea of what a serious person willing to work and learn can reasonably expect to get out of magic on the personal level.

The practice of magic causes change, both in the world and in the self. It acts in two ways. First it changes things the Magus desires and expects to change, though not always in the manner anticipated. Second, it transforms both the Magus and the world, which are in essence one, in ways totally unexpected, and often undesired, by the ego.

Those who regularly practice magic rituals designed to improve their physical health, or enhance their beauty and personality, or to succeed in business, or gain love, or heal and help others, will certainly achieve these goals to a greater or lesser extent, depending on how strongly they are desired. Magic will give you what you want, but not what you think you want. If you pretend to be altruistic, but really are more concerned with your own power and celebrity, your rituals to heal others are apt to fail.

This is not to say that those who practice magic for material ends will fail. Magic is frequently worked for the most practical and material personal reasons with complete success. But your mind must not be divided. You must not believe you want one thing when you really want something else. This split will create conflict that will render the magic ritual impotent, depriving it of focus.

Sometimes when you work a ritual to change a part of the world, you will end up changing yourself. Magic makes no distinction between inside and outside. The two are one seamless whole, and the barrier that divides you from the world around you is an illusion. For example, you may work a ritual to cause a particular person to love you. Such love magic is morally questionable but frequently practiced. Instead of changing the other person, your magic may transform your own personality and behavior so that the other, who before was indifferent to you, now finds you wildly interesting. But to your subjective perceptions, it is the other person who has changed, and is behaving differently.

The regular working of rituals has another effect that is often unsought, at least in the beginning—the expansion of human awareness on all levels. After a while, the more evolved Magus realizes that this opening of his or her perceptions is a more valuable result of ritual than the petty egocentric goals that had been pursued, and focus shifts to foster this personal growth.

The practice of magic will cause you to see the world in an entirely new way. Things that before appeared to be static will be perceived to be in motion. Everything is constantly moving and changing. Nothing remains where it was; nothing stays the same. You will also see that each thing is linked with all other things, not just by the laws of physics, but in a living way. Everything is alive and aware.

Magic will also change your view of yourself. There will no longer be "me" and "everything else." Everything else is you. You will not be able to run away from things with a clear conscience once you know in your heart that they are a part of you. Moreover, you will see that you are the center, not just of the Earth, but of the universe, which radiates away equally from you on all sides in an unendingly expanding sphere. You were not put here for the hell of it. You have a purpose which is vital to the world, as are the purposes of all living things.

The world is a great conscious being, thinking slow thoughts, aware of what transpires on her surface. She has the power to nourish and to chastise, but is by nature loving and giving. You are her child. You breathe her breath, drink her milk, play on her lap, and die in her arms. Once you know this is true with your heart as well as your head, you will never be able to hurt her again.

Magic will free you from the prison of the present. The results of your actions extending into the future will become ever more clear to you, allowing you to shape your life intelligently. This is the freedom that stems from knowledge. The more clearly you see, the less likely you are to stumble.

An entire world of thinking, feeling beings previously invisible will reveal itself. These spiritual entities, which are not composed of flesh, always surround you—they are around you even as you read these words—but your dull, material eyes are blind to them. You cannot feel their touch, hear their voices, or see their forms. As you continue the regular practice of the art of magic they will begin to caress your awareness, particularly during the actual rituals.

Yes, spirits do exist. You can prove this to yourself easily enough through the regular practice of ritual. You will find that you have a harder time convincing others of this fact, even as a person with normal sight might find it hard to persuade a man color-blind from birth of the wonderful difference between green and red. Spirits are experienced subjectively, in that someone whose consciousness has been changed by ritual can see them, while another may not see them.

In some ways, the world has been growing over the centuries. More exotic machines let us see farther into space, reach deeper inside the atom, chart the waves of the brain. In other ways, it is shrinking. There was a time when everyone knew angels existed, and was confident that miracles happened. Anything strange and wonderful might lie beyond the edge of the map labeled HERE THERE BE DRAGONS.

Writing about the spirit Nakhiel, Aleister Crowley observed:

> "Thus when we say that Nakhiel is the 'Intelligence' of the Sun, we do not mean that he lives in the Sun, but only that he has a certain rank and character; and although we can invoke him, we do not necessarily mean that he exists in the same sense of the word in which our butcher exists."
>
> —*Magick in Theory and Practice*
> Chapter 0, Dover, New York, 1976, p. 8.

I quote Crowley because, in spite of his faults, he is one of the few writers on magic to really think about what magic is and how it works. Spirits do exist. Once you begin to work magic regularly you will know this—no one will need to convince you. But precisely what spirits are is unknown to anyone. From a practical standpoint, it is enough that they interact with human beings and can be used to cause desired change on the material and mental levels. From this standpoint, they are an extension of ritual—intelligent instruments that can be directed to carry out specific actions, who will use their own initiative to a limited extent to bring desired ends to fulfillment.

WHAT YOU SHOULD NOT EXPECT FROM MAGIC

Everyone who gets into ritual magic has pretty much the same goal—he or she wants to rule the world. They may not admit it even to themselves, but they are thinking: Suppose, just suppose, I could learn to hurl lightning bolts from my fingertips, and bring mountains crumbling down, and move the Moon out of its orbit?

Magic has almost a feminine personality. She is very seductive to the newcomer. She taunts and allures with promises of power. She tickles the imagination under the chin with her possibilities. Every time the sorcerer's apprentice is about to turn away discouraged, she flips her veil and shows her smile. This is more than enough to keep those who have an innate talent for magic interested, even when they see their cherished dreams of world domination receding slowly into the mist.

Magic is seductive but not unjust. She gives far more than she takes. While she is gently pulling away the gun, she is putting a flower in its place. Instead of commanding the world, the Magus gradually learns to command personal thoughts and passions. Instead of making others see things his or her way, the Magus begins to see things their way. After a while ruling the world ceases to look like such a great idea. Too much work.

You should not expect to control others through magic. It is true that with properly executed rituals you can bring magical energy to bear on another person and change your relationship to this person in a desired way. However, everyone has a will of their own. Will is like an iceberg, in that only the tip of it shows above the surface of consciousness. If you magically push someone, they may push back. Hard. They may not even be aware that they are doing it. People who seem very weak physically and emotionally may be very strong on the unconscious level.

There is another factor to consider, which I mention only to the intelligent reader, as it is not likely to discourage fools. When you manipulate other people against their will, no matter what level you do it on, you are debasing your own soul and being far more repulsive and contemptible than you really need to be. If, on the other hand, you behave in an honorable way, you are acting in harmony with your own true nature, and may even find happiness as a result of it. Pushing other people around gives satisfaction, not happiness. Happiness has value, satisfaction does not.

Almost as alluring to the beginner as the promise of personal power is the prospect of limitless wealth. Most people have the idea that if they can master magic they can make themselves rich—otherwise, what is the good of it? Unscrupulous writers pander to this fantasy by selling books that guarantee instant money through magic, even if you have never done magic before.

No reputable New Age publisher carries this type of trash on its list. Magic is not the way to easy money. It is an art that requires discipline and dedication. Most of its rewards are intangible. A greater sense of well-being, increased confidence, a clearer appreciation of the beauty of life, better health physically and mentally—these things magic will give anyone whose heart is open to them.

You can make money with magic. Many people do, either by using it to open business opportunities for themselves and help along their careers, or by selling their magical skill to others. But it is no easier to make money by magic than by any other kind of honest, hard labor. If there is one eternal and unvarying law in this shifting universe, it is that there is no free lunch. Not ever. Not anywhere. The moment you think you are getting something for nothing, that is the time to start backpedalling.

The glamour of magic tickles all the vices, and lust is high on the list. Love magic is as old as time. A line in Virgil's *Eclogues* reads: "As this clay hardens, and as this wax melts in one and the self-same fire, even so let Daphnis melt with love for me, to others' love be hard." (*Eclogue VIII, ll.* 80-1). This is perfectly good magic, but questionable morality. What right has Amaryllis to tell Daphnis who he may and may not love? If she succeeds in binding the love of Daphnis, does she really think he will ever be truly content and happy during their future years together? Is it not more likely that he will end up hating her, even though he cannot leave her? But perhaps she is thinking only about herself, the glory of conquest, the pride of possession, and does not care whether Daphnis is happy, so long as she has him. Whatever this feeling may be, it would be difficult to characterize it as love, although it usually passes under this name.

You can use magic to find a lover, but this may be done in an intelligent or an unintelligent way. If you are seeking love, you should invite it in a form that is in harmony with your essential nature. First, you may need to use ritual to discover what your nature is. Few people see themselves clearly. Often they are attracted to someone with the qualities they admire but lack in themselves. If you already have a person in mind, you should use the Art to transform yourself and your circumstances so that the other will seek out your company, rather than trying to compel the prospective lover.

Following closely on the heels of power, money, and sex in the list of magical seductions is fame. Who is so callow among us that he or she has not fantasized about taking up the magic wand and performing a wonder here, a miracle there, to the cheering and applause of gathered thousands? Suppose you could save someone terminally ill from cancer—not just anyone, but someone really worthwhile and important. Or suppose you could ignite the Olympic flame at the next Olympic Games with a muttered word of power and a scowl. Imagine the publicity!

Sorry, magic does not work that way. It may have something to do with the fact that magic depends upon belief; or that magic transcends natural laws and is therefore unpredictable; or that magic is directed by an awareness in the unconscious called the Higher Self. If we cannot be certain that it has a moral code, at least we can confidently state it has a sense of humor. Whatever the reason, whenever a self-proclaimed "master of the occult arts" publicly performs a miracle, the miracle is absolutely certain to fail.

I have a confession to make—I have never levitated, walked on water, restored life to the dead, lit fires with my mind, turned myself into a wolf, or divined a winning lottery number. Maybe this makes me an inferior Magus. There are certainly enough people out there who do claim to be able to perform these wonders. However, I have not seen them do so. Am I willing to say such feats are impossible? Of course not; such a statement would be rash. But I have not done them, and have never seen them done.

On the other hand, I have done a variety of things that would strike most people as unusual. I have communicated with spirits, for example, in a variety of ways. I do not know precisely what spirits are, but I know that I have talked with and touched a number of them.

Also, I have made myself invisible. This may require a brief explanation. To be magically invisible does not mean other people do not see you; it means that they do not notice you. This is a strange, but at the same time an oddly liberating feeling. Also, I have left my body and looked back upon it—but precisely where I was when I was astrally traveling, or whether I was in any dimension of space at all, is a matter for conjecture.

In not one of these personal experiments did I tell a single soul beforehand what I was going to do. This makes them difficult to verify by the scientific method. However, silence was needed if they were to have any chance of success. The one way to be certain a ritual will fail is to brag about it beforehand to those unconnected with its working. In magic silence is not just a matter of discretion, but practical necessity.

WHY RITUAL MAGIC IS IMPORTANT IN YOUR LIFE

Everyone is searching for the meaning of life. Not so much life in general, but of their own life. They want to know why they exist and what they are supposed to do with existence. They want to feel productive and fulfilled. Most of all, they want to be happy.

Living in a modern city is like being trapped in a great machine, whirled round by cogs and gears, shunted from place to place in repetitious patterns, never given an explanation for what is happening. The machine allows only one option to the poor rats racing madly inside its works. Either they get into step with the gears and push rods, or they are ground into hamburger. The machine has no time for pity.

Those who succumb to the remorseless song of steel become slaves, not to other men, but to the cold, calculating god of contemporary society—a god I have christened Mekanos—whose only criterion is efficiency. Never mind that a job serves no human function, so long as it is efficiently done. Never mind that it does nothing for the soul, so long as it is in lockstep with the social order. I am not preaching ideology here—Mekanos, like Janus, has two faces: one Uncle Sam, the other Karl Marx.

Those who opt out of the system or who cannot manage to march in step with it, are destroyed. For a while they may enjoy frolicking between the assembly lines while their more timid peers toil away. But sooner or later their feet slip, and like Charlie Chaplin in *Modern Times* are consumed by the social process. They end up in prisons, in mental hospitals, or in coffins.

Magic is the doorway out of the machine. It is not a door that leads to another physical place because the machine is a state of mind, and no one can escape from themselves. Rather, it opens a new awareness of the world where dreams can happen, and where human actions do have meaning. It opens on hope and purpose.

People are not fools. If they are told that the world is gray and heartless, that their lives are insignificant, that the dreams they dream and the feelings they feel are trivial, and if they believe this lie, they will experience a sense of futility. But if they realize that they are important to the world, indeed its very heart, and that every thought and feeling they have is significant, not only in their own lives but to all life, and if it is pointed out to them that, at least potentially, they have complete and utter control over their own lives, they will experience a great sense of freedom.

Ritual is a mechanism for changing all four levels of being: physical, emotional, mental, and spiritual. We all know that our feelings affect our physical health and condition. We know that our minds, both the part we see and the part we do not see, control our feelings. What many do not realize is that there is a fourth level of spirit that determines the state of our minds. Normal activities deny the existence of this level of spirit, thereby denying access to it. If spirit is out of balance, the mind is affected, giving a jaundiced assessment of the world. If the mind is warped, the feelings will be unhappy. If the emotions are hurtful, health will suffer.

Through magic a channel of awareness can be opened between the spirit or Higher Self, and the ego or ordinary self, allowing the Higher Self, which always knows who it is and what it wants to do, to direct and shape the ego, thereby restoring a balance to the emotions and improving health. And because these four levels are intimately connected in a reciprocal way, improved health can restore optimism, which can in turn provide a rosier outlook on life.

The greatest benefit of ritual may be, not its limitless power of transformation, but the way it allows those who practice it to perceive value in things they already possess, whether these are the forests and lakes around them, or the people in their lives. To see the world magically is to see it in color, where before everything was black and white.

MAGIC, THE ALTERNATE VIEWPOINT

Where in the world is magic? It is not in science, which denies the reality and value of anything not amenable to the scientific method. It is not in religion. The Church has historically looked upon magic as devilish, and in modern times regards it as a pathetic delusion. It is not in business, which has no money to waste on such frivolous pursuits as transformation of the soul. Neither is magic to be found in the universities or public schools, except as a footnote in the study of history and primitive cultures.

Magic is an outcast. Like all outcasts it is regarded as disreputable and viewed with suspicion by the bastions of the establishment. Bored people with time on their hands sometimes take up the practice of ritual as an amusement, and quickly abandon it. Those who seriously practice ritual in their daily lives maintain a prudent silence. True, sorcerers are no longer burned at the stake or hung, as they were in former ages. Even so, it does not do for those in sensitive occupations—for the police, doctors or commercial airline pilots, for example—to let it be generally known that they conduct magical rituals. Such an admission ensures that they will be labeled as the lunatic fringe, and deemed unsuitable for positions of responsibility. If they do not lose their jobs, they can at least be certain they will never be promoted.

Attitudes are changing. The expansion of New Age subjects into all walks of life has carried magic along with it. Magic has ceased to be a taboo subject and instead, has become a curiosity. Everyone is interested in magic, but they are afraid to admit that their interest is serious. Given half a chance, they would attend seminars and university lectures to learn the practice of rituals, if such schools existed, and if no one would laugh at them. Though magic is now being talked about, it is far from being accepted. It still requires personal courage to commit wholeheartedly to the study of the oldest and most sacred of the arts.

The question most often asked by readers of my books is: How can I find a teacher? It is difficult to answer specifically, as it depends upon the interest of the individual and the region in which he or she is living. Most groups devoted to ritual magic neither need nor want new members. The relationship between teacher and pupil is intensely personal, more so in magic than in any other field of study. It requires an unqualified devotion on both sides and complete trust. Regrettably, there are innumerable individuals and groups who teach, or pretend to teach, ceremonial magic for money. While they can teach the mechanics of the Art, which are basic and more or less universal, they cannot impart the living soul of magic that gives the Art its meaning.

I usually advise anyone wanting to learn magic to read as much as possible so that they will not be ignorant of the mechanics, and then to practice ritual in their own lives. Even if that initial practice is flawed technically, it has great value because it begins to open up the mind to directions from the level of spirit, and expands the perceptions of the world. At the same time, they should be attending lectures and seminars on New Age subjects in their area, keeping their eyes open for notices of clubs or groups being formed that have an occult focus, and following such disciplines as yoga, meditation, Tai Chi and other martial arts. In this way useful social contacts can be made.

Rituals can be conducted by an individual in solitude or with others in a group. Group ritual is favored by most people, who draw support from the other members of the circle. It is easiest to learn the basics of ceremonial magic through imitation. Those who work alone often become discouraged when they find themselves pouring large amounts of energy into their rituals while seemingly getting little or nothing in return. After working ceremonial magic awhile, you become aware of the long-term cycles of the mind that extend over a period of many months, cycles of energy and lethargy, of enthusiasm and despair. Group practice helps individuals get through the low points in their cycles.

There are two main groups practicing the Western magical tradition. The more numerous are the Witchcraft, Druid, and related pagan circles that incorporate magic into their ritual worship of Nature. The rituals worked by them may be called natural magic. Emphasis is placed upon the magical properties of places, stones, trees, herbs, and foods. Witchcraft has descended at least in part from the folk magic of the Saxons and Celts.

The less numerous groups practice a more abstract ceremonial magic that has its roots in Neoplatonism and Jewish mysticism. They deal in words, symbols, and numbers, and work more directly through the mediation of spirits to accomplish their purposes. This type of ritual may be called high magic or theurgy, and is deemed by some—erroneously, it seems to me—to be more potent.

Perhaps the reason theurgy is less widely practiced than Witchcraft is because it lacks an underlying religious structure. Witchcraft is foremostly a nature religion that uses magic to integrate the human soul with the Soul of the World. At its best, it is a gentle, earthy experience of great beauty and power. Theurgy is less concerned with worship and cannot be called a religion. Its ultimate objective is the alchemical Great Work of soul liberation through which the individual begins to act with full power and awareness in the world for the realization of personal destiny.

Ultimately, Witchcraft and theurgy have the same objective, which is the release and application of human potential through magic for the purpose of life fulfillment. This goal is not achieved all at once. Perhaps it is never achieved to its fullest possible degree—who can say how awesomely powerful a fully realized human being would be? Rather, it is achieved through small victories that make life a little more worth living.

Those who use ritual magic in their daily lives have grown disenchanted with the sterility of modern industrialized Western society. They want something more in their world than the laws of physics and the profit motive, and have not been able to find it within the existing network of social groups and religious organizations. They are people who feel they have lost control of the evolution of their souls and want to win it back. They seek fulfillment and purpose. They look for a viable mechanism for change, not only on the physical but on the emotional and mental levels as well.

Although the practitioners of magic make up a kind of secret underground, they are not drawn from any one stratum of society. They come from all backgrounds and walks of life. There are Christian occult churches, temples of the Kabbalah with strongly Orthodox opinions, feminist Wicca covens worshiping God as a woman, lesbian and gay circles, Druidic brotherhoods, groups based on the writing of the anarchistic Aleister Crowley, groups founded on the Victorian principles of the Order of the Golden Dawn, survivalists, racists, ecologists, animal rights activists—all using ritual to further their diverse goals. And I am referring here only to those who use predominantly Western magic. Groups based upon Zen and Buddhist techniques, Tao, yoga, and tantra are even more numerous.

I leave out of the discussion the groups classed as Satanic in the popular media. There are very few actually working magic in a serious way for outright evil purposes. Magic is a discipline that requires years of dedication, even when it is used to hurt rather than to heal. Most Satanists are mere posturers who adopt Satanic imagery as a fashion statement, or use it to embellish criminal acts which they would commit in any case. It provides a focus for the media but usually has nothing directly to do with whatever atrocity has drawn the attention. If torture, mutilation, murder, and other crimes are being committed specifically to raise magical power for some desired end, this is truly Satanic, in the loose sense of the word, but this is rare.

WHAT RITUAL MAGIC ENTAILS

By now you may be impatiently asking yourself what ritual magic is, and how to perform it. I want to point out before beginning that it is impossible to fully describe such an extensive subject in this small essay. That is why so many excellent books have been written, books such as *The Golden Dawn*, edited from the secret papers of the magical Order of the Golden Dawn by the late Israel Regardie; and *The Magickal Philosophy*, written by two members of the occult society Aurum Solis, Melita Denning and Osborne Phillips—both of which I heartily recommend. That is why I have written *The New Magus* and *Rune Magic*. All that can be done here is to provide a taste of what ritual magic consists of, as practiced by hundreds of thousands of people in the modern world, and describe some of the universal techniques that form its foundation.

There is general agreement among scholars that all drama began as magical ritual. The hunter who dressed in a stagskin and danced around the fire, pantomiming his own death, was working hunting magic against the living beasts in the forest. At the same time, he was performing a play before an audience made up secondarily of his fellow hunters, but primarily of the gods.

This magical element predominated in the sacred Mystery plays enacted in ancient Egypt and Greece. It was only when Aeschylus and his contemporaries in the sixth century B.C. began to elaborate on the narrative aspect of the presentation that it took precedence over the original magical purpose. Drama became entertainment, and the audience forgot its original function, which was to bring about change in the world by magical means.

Externally every ritual consists of a fixed set of gestures, movements, and words within a deliberately circumscribed arena or stage. Common features are song, chants, dance, special postures, and breathing. Some or all of these aspects may be internalized—they are still done, but done in the imagination. Since the audience for magic is the Higher Self and the discarnate spirits, it is not strictly necessary to externalize the ritual, although this is usually found to be easier and more effective for the practitioners.

Almost by definition, ritual actions are designed to be repeated in the same sequence and manner many times without variation. It is debatable whether a ritual performed only once can even be called a ritual. Rituals gather power through repetition. Were a ritual to be fundamentally changed each time it were conducted, it would remain impotent. It is my personal opinion, based on experience, that the spiritual awareness or awarenesses interacting with the ritual learn through repetition to recognize it as intended for them and *come when called*, just as a dog will only respond to its name after it has become familiar with it.

The perception of discarnate Intelligences is not the same as that of human beings. Usually the human and spirit worlds do not interact. Ritual is like a door opening in the middle of the air in the spirit world, the world of magic. If the doorway materializes regularly and often enough, the spirits will come to expect it, and will gather in anticipation of its opening. Bear in mind that this is only a metaphor for the response I have observed in spirits. The same virtue of repetition holds true even in acts of magic that apparently do not involve other spiritual awarenesses. Repetition increases the force and the speed of the ritual outcome.

The underlying premise of magical ritual is that if you represent a circumstance, or act out an event in your mind, it will come to pass in the world. This is what James G. Frazer, in his monumental work *The Golden Bough,* calls the Law of Similarity: "From the Law of Similarity, the magician infers that he can produce any effect he desires merely by imitating it." (*The Golden Bough,* abridged edition, Chapter III. Macmillan, New York, 1951, p. 12.)

Frazer uses the familiar example of a sorcerer who pricks a doll, made in the image of an enemy, with pins to cause injury to his foe. He speaks of material links with the victim's nail parings, hair, and such—but largely ignores the essential connecting link, the mind of the sorcerer. It cannot be emphasized too strongly that magic acts in and through the mind. The external elements of ritual are only sensory aids for the benefit of the magician.

You will need a place set aside for your rituals where you can feel safe, at peace with your emotions, secure from interruption and distraction. You must be able to concentrate completely on one purpose during the time of the ritual. If the person in the next apartment is blasting the stereo, and this gets on your nerves, it is a poor ritual place. You must conduct your rituals at a time when this distraction does not exist, or find another place.

The ritual place need not be large, but must be comfortable. A small mat is useful if the floor is uncarpeted. Some practitioners use a chair, but I find this to be an encumbrance, because in ritual it is necessary to move about, sit, then move about again; and a chair only gets in the way.

As far as possible, everything in the ritual place that is not in harmony with the ritual purpose, whatever it may be at that time, should be minimized or excluded. Everything that supports the ritual purpose should be prominently present, with the proviso that clutter is always a distraction.

Loose clothing should be worn. Belts, shoes, rings, watches, jewelry, and other constricting apparel should be removed. It is useful, though not absolutely necessary, to have a special garment set aside specifically for ritual magic that is comfortable and simple. It is also useful to take a warm bath before each ritual, making it a part of the preliminary purification. This relaxes the body and releases tension, and allows you to present yourself before the gods and your own higher awareness in a pure state, once you have learned to combine the cleansing of the mind with the washing of the flesh. This consists in allowing all the emotional and mental dirt of the day to dissolve away into the warm water and follow it down the drain.

After you have bathed and appareled, it is best to you sit down in the ritual place for a few minutes or so and prepare yourself by creating an inner tranquillity. You need not think about the ritual itself during this period; your unconscious mind will automatically be preparing for it. Also, it is useful to set aside a half hour or so after the ritual to wind down and return your mind to an everyday state of awareness. It is a poor practice to conduct rituals so late at night that you are exhausted immediately after you finish and at once fall asleep. This is guaranteed to give you nightmares. If you do happen to have bad dreams after ritual work, do not worry about them—they are only dreams, and have no power to directly harm you.

Elaborate rituals are not necessary. I keep mine as simple as possible. When a ritual becomes too complex, it is an effort just to remember all the elements, let alone practice it. Also, when rituals consume long periods of time—more than an hour or so—they tend to be exhausting and to lose their focus.

Whether you practice ritual magic once a day or once a week, you will need to keep a written record of your activities, both your purposes and methods, and their results. Writing down a ritual ensures that it is clearly conceived. It is itself a mental rehearsal for the ritual that will follow.

The benefit of recording results is that it allows the Magus to perceive effects and transformations that may be quite slow and subtle, and to mark their direction of progress. This heads off the unfortunate event of a sudden realization that the work is going in the wrong direction, and permits corrections to be made early, before the harm is done. An accurate record can also reveal a great deal about the unseen mechanism of the mind of the Magus, who is then able to use this knowledge to advantage in future rituals. Most occultists also recommend that dreams be recorded during the time of major workings (repeated rituals conducted over a span of weeks or months), for the insight they yield into the effects of the ritual process.

BASIC INSTRUMENTS OF RITUAL

The basic framework of Western magic is made up of a few surprisingly simple instruments that function on the astral plane (another way of saying in the imagination). Usually they have their material correspondents. As the physical instrument is manipulated in the physical ritual place, the astral instrument follows and reflects its action in the astral temple. It is possible to use the astral instruments without using the material, but this requires a more developed visual imagination, and is seldom as effective.

The essential instruments of ritual are the circle; the altar; the lamp; the four elemental symbols for Fire, Air, Water and Earth; the wand; the sword; the ring; the robe; the knife; and the materials used for purification, consisting of water, salt, and fire.

Many other instruments and materials, such as incense, flowers, colored lights, music, cakes, wine, symbols, images, and so on, are used to affect the mind, but the ones in the previous paragraph are the most essential. Also used are non-material tools such as words, chants, hand and body gestures, postures, and visualization of incorporeal structures such as the chakras and pentagrams. There is not nearly enough space here to discuss everything employed in ritual magic, but I will briefly touch on the most important tools.

Circle

The magic circle is drawn in the astral world about the Magus and the place where the ritual is worked. It forms a division between the magical place and the ordinary world, setting the interior space apart. This allows the region inside the circle to hold a heightened charge of magical potency, and because it is a pure space devoted to worship and magic, it permits the manifestation of spiritual Intelligences that could not be readily perceived in the ordinary environment. The circle also acts as a barrier that protects the Magus from the intrusion of discordant, chaotic forces that seek to disrupt communications with higher spiritual beings, or even to harm the Magus in emotional and physical ways.

The circle is always inscribed from the inside, ideally from the center, in a sunwise direction, and visualized as a glowing or flaming band of light that sustains itself in the air at the level of the heart. Often a corresponding physical circle of the same radius is marked on the floor of the chamber beforehand; but the magic circle does not actually exist until it is made in the astral by a deliberate act of will. For convenience, the circle is made of a size great enough to enclose the ritual place. A single ritualist, if working without an altar in a confined space, might project a circle of six feet in diameter. With an altar at the center, the circle might be nine feet in diameter to permit movement around the altar. Since the circle is drawn in the astral, it can be made larger than the actual physical chamber.

Whatever its size, the circle should always be large enough to comfortably hold all who work within it. Because the circle is magically real, even though immaterial, it must never be casually broken. It is extended from the heart center of the Magus clockwise from the point of the right index finger, or the point of the wand, sword, or knife. It should be reabsorbed at the end of the ritual in through the left index finger, or magical instrument held in the left hand, by retracing it widdershins—against the course of the Sun. It must never be stepped through, although this is a common mistake among occultists. To disregard the substantiality of the circle is to weaken it, and so render it a less useful tool.

Altar

At the center of the circle is placed the altar, which magically represents the center of the universe and the center of the self. It is the working surface of ritual, the focus of awareness and power. When there is no space for a material altar, one may be visualized in the astral. The altar is square on top, cubic or doubly-cubic in dimension, and should be made of, or contain, natural stone. All these aspects symbolize that the altar is the material foundation that supports the work; it is the fixed place, the earthly buttress, where power is manifested and made actual in the world.

Lamp

The spiritual focus of the circle is the flame of the lamp, which is always lit during rituals, and which resides in the middle of the altar top. The absolute magical center of the circle is the invisible point where the flame of the lamp tapers up and vanishes into infinity. Usually a ceramic or metal oil lamp is used, but a candle is acceptable. Some groups maintain a perpetual flame on their altars. This is beyond the reach of small circles or individuals, but the flame should be maintained without failing in the astral temple in the mind of each ritualist. This is the true occult perpetual lamp.

The flame is the focus of the awareness of those working the ritual. They direct their prayers to it and meditate upon it. The point at which it disappears into infinity marks the doorway in the Vëil of Unknowing, which the ritual is designed to open. The flame should be conceived by the Magus as burning in the center of his or her being, throwing its light across the circle of self. When the circle is filled with light, the self is purified and exalted.

Purification

Once the lamp has been lit and the circle made, the interior of the circle is purged with the materials of purification, which represent one or more of the occult elements. Some groups purify with all four elements, or with the three active elements of Fire, Water, and Air (Earth is regarded as a mixture of these three), as described in *The New Magus*. In my personal rituals I often use the ancient materials of cleansing: salt, water, and flame. Salt symbolizes elemental Earth, water elemental Water, and the flame combines elemental Fire and Air in the form of a smoking candle or incense stick.

The salt, previously blessed by prayer and consecrated to its purpose, is cast in small pinches sunwise around the circle at the four cardinal points of South, West, North, and East. The water, likewise consecrated, is sprinkled from the fingertips in a similar manner at the four quarters. The flame is waved three times in the air at each of the corners of the circle. Usually the entire act of cleansing is accompanied by prayer.

Remember that you are cleaning the house of the spirit so that the light of the spirit will descend and reside within it. This is a sacred act. It has been said by other writers that purification is the most important part of any ritual. It sets the stage for what is to follow. When done negligently, the work that comes after it will likely be futile, because it will lack a solid foundation.

Elemental Symbols

Much of magic is done through the mediation of the four occult elements, Fire, Air, Water, and Earth. They determine both the type of energy that accomplishes the work and the avenue through which it acts. For this reason a clear understanding and proper use of the elements is vital in ritual. Each element is represented by its own material symbol, which is placed atop the altar beside the lamp in the appropriate elemental quarter. If a ritual concerns only one element, its symbol is placed on the altar alone; if all four elements are involved, all four symbols are present.

Fire is embodied in a short rod about nine inches long. This has a very specific design in the Golden Dawn magical system, but the details are not really necessary. It is the essential shape of the rod that is most important. The nature of elemental Fire is in accord with this strongly phallic symbol.

Air is embodied in a short dagger. Again, it is the associations of the blade—its flashing quickness, its piercing quality, its brightness—that are important, not details of the hilt and so on. The difference in tone between the rod and the dagger says much about the essential difference between elemental Fire and Air.

Water is embodied in a cup or chalice. It should be rounded and womblike, enclosing and protective. It is also more harmonious if the cup is made of a watery, or at least a natural, material. Blue handblown glass is good, or earth-tone ceramic.

Earth is embodied in the disk or pentacle. This is a flat disk painted with Earth colors. Ideally it should be made of clay or stone. Usually it is of wood. It must not be too large to conveniently hold in the hand—four inches in diameter is a good size, because four is a material, earthy number.

So far as I know, the use of elemental symbols originated with the Victorian Order of the Golden Dawn in the last century, and received its inspiration from the symbols of the lesser arcana—the number cards—of the Tarot. Specific, formal symbols of the four elements were not used in medieval times, and are not strictly necessary. However, the employment of these symbols has become almost universal in modern magic, and they can be very useful. It is important that they be made to harmonize with the sensibilities of the one who will actually use them, not merely according to some arbitrary standard.

Robe

The Magus is usually robed in a special garment used only for ritual purposes. Since it is kept pure and apart, and since it is only worn after the Magus has bathed and purified his or her own body, donning it is akin to putting on a cloak of light. It can be helpful both in raising the consciousness to a higher awareness of spirit, and also to shield the Magus from discordant influences. The robe must be comfortable, and more importantly must feel appropriate to its wearer. I prefer white because of its benign associations. Colors tend to have specific emotions bound up with them, and these are not merely social commonplaces, but run to the primal roots of human response. For example, red is always a color of violence and rage, no matter what a particular political propagandist or French designer might wish it to be. Any loose, comfortable clothing can become the ritual garb, provided it is set aside and treated with reverence.

Wand

The quintessential magical tool in the minds of most people is the wand. This is made by the Magus to project the power of will. In fact, it becomes the physical representation of his or her magical will. It should be made of wood, about as thick as the thumb and as long as the space between the fingertips and the elbow. Some woods are favored for the wand—hazel is traditional. Oak is also good, being the wood of Zeus and therefore the traditional attractor of lightning. Ideally, the wand should be cut and fashioned by the Magus, as it becomes the most intensely personal tool of the Art and is used for virtually everything. Over time, it will gather a magical charge through use that is clearly perceptible when it is held.

Sword

Less useful, but still necessary for high magic or theurgy which involves chaotic spirits, is the sword. This is similar in its functioning to the wand, but whereas the wand has a neutral nature, the sword is overtly offensive, projecting power to dominate and hurt. It is supposed to be made by the Magus, but I hazard to say that not one in a thousand occultists who possesses the magic sword has actually fashioned the blade by hand. It is considered acceptable to procure a short sword, or long knife, and after thoroughly purifying it, consecrate it by anointing and prayer to its magical purpose. I use an old British army bayonet myself, which is shaped as a sword, hilt and all, and find it effective—perhaps especially so due to its military associations.

Athame

A tool used by Witches that combines the functioning of both wand and sword is the athame, or magical knife. It is an all-purpose instrument, used for making the material objects of ritual and also for projecting power. Some Witches even use it in their cooking! They explain that since magic embraces all of life, cooking is an integral part of their Art and this is no profanation.

The magical knife is quite old. In medieval times it was divided into two—a knife with a white hilt, used for all common purposes; a knife with a black hilt, used for drawing magic circles and compelling spirits. This distinction is still frequently observed by modern Witches. The white and black-hilted knives are in some ways analogous to the wand and sword of high magic.

Descriptions for the making of the white-and black-hilted knives occur in one of the oldest Western grimoires, the *Greater Key of Solomon* (Mathers' edition, B. II, Ch. viii). They entail the slaughter of innocent animals, a poor way to begin a spiritual quest. I give the above reference only to show the ancient lineage of the Witch's athame, not as a prescription to be followed. In fact, many of the techniques in the ancient grimoires, while they contain kernels of sense, are needlessly involved and difficult. In modern times, magic is much more straightforward, and as a consequence, more practical.

Ring

The final essential instrument that I mean to mention here is the ring. This fits over the index finger of the right hand, and acts as a sort of magical magnetic coil, magnifying the force of the will that passes along the index finger. It also serves as a miniature representation of the magic circle, and protects its wearer from harm. Perhaps the best form of the ring is a plain gold or silver band, a bit broader than usual. By it the Magus is wedded to the Art of magic. It is customary to inscribe the ring with names of power such as the Hebrew IHVH, the divine Tetragrammaton.

Several different rings may be made for specific purposes. For example, an individual spirit can be made to reside in a ring, and its power utilized when the ring is put on. The ancient Greek magician Apollonius of Tyana possessed seven rings named after the seven planets, given to him as a gift by Iarchas, leader of the Brahmans of India. He wore each of these rings in rotation on the day of the week related to its planet. As is true of all the instruments, there is no exact pattern for the magic ring. The shape and choice of inscription depends on its use, and the personality of its maker.

THE GOAL OF RITUAL

The ultimate goal of ritual magic is fulfillment. As is true with most ultimates, it is seldom, if ever, reached. The degree to which it is approached signifies the success or failure of the practice of magic in the life of an individual. When ritual is sincerely and regularly practiced, in most cases there will be a benefit. Sometimes the improvement, from both an objective and subjective perspective, is remarkable. Magic can improve health and appearance, increase confidence and a sense of self-worth, remove obstacles hindering the progress of a life, and bring about a spiritual rebirth.

All lesser improvements tend toward the creation of a total, fulfilled, self-actualized life. They are pieces of a puzzle that make up a single perfect image. In order to impress this fact upon the mind of the newcomer into magic groups, both ancient and modern, it is very common for an initiation ceremony to be conducted. The initiation represents in brief the highest goal of magic. It is a magic ritual designed to realize that purpose in the months and years that follow.

Usually the initiate undergoes, in one form or another, a symbolic death and rebirth. The death emphasizes that the old world of confusion, ignorance and helplessness is being left behind. The rebirth stands for the new life as a totally realized human soul, able to act with complete freedom in any circumstance. This transformation is further driven home by assigning the initiate a new name.

The initiation ceremony is only a representation of what the members of the circle, and the initiate, wish to have happen. It is up to the Magus to make this transformation occur in his or her life through hard work and dedication. Although success is never complete, change can be profound. The result is simply a better human being from every angle.

One technique used in the West to bring about this soul transformation is a ritual communication with what, for want of a better name, has been called the Holy Guardian Angel. This is simply the higher spiritual awareness that concerns itself in the affairs of a single human being. It might as easily be called the Higher Self, or the personal God. It is the consciousness that cares enough about the happiness of a person to take the trouble to help.

Every person sees his or her Guardian Angel in a unique way.

The prophets of the major religions often don the mask of Guardian Angel, and are conceived differently by each worshiper, and so become personal to each, guiding and sustaining the individual through difficulties. The difference is that in magic, this communication is sought and established in a deliberate way, not merely to gain support in times of pain and doubt, but to transform the soul of the Magus on a permanent basis.

As I mentioned earlier, this is the highest goal. Magic is often worked for more humble and pragmatic reasons, and there is nothing wrong with this. But it should be understood that all improvements in a life, if they really are improvements and not mere illusions, tend toward the perfection of that life. Those actively interested in pursuing the conversation of the Guardian Angel should read *The Book of the Sacred Magic of Abramelin the Mage,* translated by one of the founders of the Golden

Dawn, S. L. MacGregor Mathers (Dover, New York, 1975); the *Sacred Magician* by Georges Chevalier (Paladin, Suffolk, 1976), which is a diary of the working described in *Abramelin*; and chapter 29 of my own *New Magus* (Llewellyn, St. Paul, Minnesota, 1988), which looks at the process from a theoretical, as well as a practical, standpoint.

RITUAL TO AWAKEN MAGICAL AWARENESS

Everyone learns best by doing. The ritual described below is representative of the rituals worked in modern magic. It should be used as a general pattern indicating the essential elements and sequence of rituals, and will also, I hope, be of some value in awakening a magical perception of the world, which in no small measure consists of just being aware that it is possible to see the world in a new way. Because few people reading this essay will possess a full set of ritual tools, I have designed it so that it does not require any instruments except the flame. It can be worked in any private place where there is half an hour of quiet.

Wear loose, comfortable clothing of neutral colors. Take off your watch, jewelry, shoes, and anything that hinders a free circulation of blood or irritates the skin. It is best if, before beginning, you bathe, or at least wash your hands and face. Remember, you are invoking a spiritual awareness into the temple of your body.

Place a candle on a low table, such as a bedside table, a plantstand, or other support, so that the candle is just below waist level, and light the candle. Take a few minutes to collect your emotions. When you feel inner tranquillity, stand facing the south with the candle in front of you. Raise your arms wide and lift up your head in the traditional posture of invocation. Look into infinity and focus your attention upon an imaginary distant star overhead. Speak this cleansing prayer to whatever is your concept of the highest divinity:

Have mercy upon me, O God.
Blot out my transgressions.
Wash me thoroughly from my iniquities
And cleanse me from my sins.
Purge me with hyssop, and I shall be clean;
Wash me, and I shall be as white as snow.
Create in me a clean heart,
And renew a right spirit within me.
Thou, who art the Crown
(touch your forehead with your right index finger)
And the Kingdom,
(touch your groin)
The Power
(touch your left shoulder)
And the Glory,
(touch your right shoulder)
And the everlasting Law,

(touch your heart center)

Amen.

(point at the flame)

As you speak this cleansing prayer, visualize a cascade of clear, sparkling water falling upon your head and body and refreshing you while washing away all your cares.

Turn sunwise on your own axis and mentally project from your extended right index finger a blazing circle of white light that hovers in the astral shadow of the place where the ritual is being conducted. Try to picture this circle clearly at the level of your heart, the energy that composes it growing out from your heart center down your right arm and out your fingertip. Be sure to join the end of the circle with the beginning in your mind. If necessary, mentally expand the circle as you project it to include the ritual place.

Speak these words as you project the circle:

From my heart of being I extend this flaming circle of power. Let no evil or discordant influence enter herein nor abide within its boundary.

Once again facing the south, stand with your feet together and your arms spread wide, making a cross with your body. Visualize a massive column of red flame rising from the Earth just beyond the limit of the circle and extending up into infinity. Concentrate upon it and speak these words:

Before me Michael, Lord of Flame, the lion of the south.

Without moving, visualize behind you in the north a similar column of yellow fire. Speak these words:

Behind me Raphael, Lord of Air, the angel of the north.

Visualize in the west a column of blue fire beyond the circle. Speak these words:

On my right hand Gabriel, Lord of Water, the eagle of the west.

Visualize in the east a column of green fire. Speak the words:

On my left hand Uriel, Lord of Earth, the bull of the east.

Then say:

The four surround me,
(raise your hands slightly above the level of your head)
Fire above,
(lower your hands to the level of your waist)
Water below;

(bring your palms together in a prayer gesture over your heart)

I am the heart of the four, I am the center of the universe.

Visualize a cross of light radiating from its point of intersection in your heart center. The vertical beam of the cross is red, and runs between your feet and through the top of your head to infinity. The horizontal beam running under your shoulders is blue. The horizontal beam which enters your chest between your clasped palms and exits your back is yellow. Your heart center blazes with a clear white light that fills your entire body as if it were a glass vessel.

Sit upon the floor before the candle and contemplate the flame. Let your breathing be light and regular. Be aware of the turbulence in the air and wait for it to be completely stilled, so that the flame rises straight up in a cone with hardly a flicker. You should be far enough away so that your breath does not disturb it. Try to become tangibly aware of the body and substance of the flame from all angles. Involve yourself with it. Imagine that you are surrounded by it, and that it does not discomfort you in the least. The sensation is like being encased in an upwardly flowing teardrop of sunlight.

Gradually let your breaths grow deeper and longer without forcing them or straining yourself. Remain relaxed. As you inhale fully, hold your breath for five or 10 seconds and focus your awareness solely upon the uppermost point of the flame, where it vanishes into nothingness. Try to focus like a microscope of infinite power ever more finely upon the exact place where the transition between flame and space occurs.

When you release your breath, let your mind once again embrace the entire body of the flame. The next time you inhale, again halt your breath for a few seconds and focus upon the tip of the flame. Try at each stoppage of breath to get ever closer to the elusive vanishing point.

It is vital to the success of this technique that you do not strain yourself by trying to breathe too deeply, or retain your breath too long. If you end up short of breath *that* is where your attention will be, and the whole purpose will be defeated. It may require several practices before a light, effortless rhythm of breaths and retentions can be established. I cannot stress enough that the actual length of the retention, or the number of retentions, is of no importance whatsoever. Only the rhythmic shifting of your awareness from the body of the flame to its vanishing point is of significance. At each focus upon the tip of the flame, try for at least a fraction of a second to direct all your perception and will upon the dimensionless margin where it disappears out of the universe.

After a few dozen breaths, and before you even start to grow tired either mentally or physically, stand up facing the south. Raise your arms in the gesture of invocation, saying in a calm but confident voice:

> *I give thanks for the successful fulfillment of this ritual to awaken a true perception of the Light of Spirit.*

Extending your left index finger to the magic circle in the south, rotate upon your axis widdershins—to the left—and mentally reabsorb the ring of astral flame into your heart center as you speak these words:

> *I hereby absorb this flaming circle of power into my heart of being, returning this ritual place to its former level.*

Facing the south once again, cross yourself as you did in the opening of the ritual, speaking these words:

> *May the grace of the Light*
> *Guide and protect me,*
> *Who art the Crown*
> (touch your forehead)
> *And the Kingdom,*
> (groin)
> *The Power*
> (left shoulder)

And the Glory,
(right shoulder)
And the everlasting Law,
(touch your heart center)
Amen.
(point at the flame)

Clap your hands together four times and spread your arms wide with your fingers splayed, saying:

This ritual for awakening an awareness of Light is well and truly completed.

Blow out the candle and relax for a few minutes before turning your energies to any other task. Do not try to go over the ritual in your mind. Just be passive and let it work itself upon your unconscious.

I chose this ritual because it is not dangerous, and so requires no banishing formula. Since it is worked primarily in the astral by visualization it can be done without magical instruments. However, it is still a very potent ritual. If you work it each day for several weeks, you should notice subtle yet unmistakable changes in your awareness. The ritual purpose has deliberately been left unspecified in order to promote those transformations most natural to each individual. A general stirring of higher perceptions, as well as an increase in vitality, are to be expected. Other effects will depend on the personality and abilities of the person using the ritual. For a lasting change, it should be worked regularly for several months.

STAY IN TOUCH

On the following pages you will find some of the books now available on related subjects. Your book dealer stocks most of these and will stock new titles in the Llewellyn series as they become available. We urge your patronage.

To obtain our full catalog write for our bimonthly news magazine/catalog, *Llewellyn's New Worlds of Mind and Spirit*. A sample copy is free, and it will continue coming to you at no cost as long as you are an active mail customer. Or you may subscribe for just $10.00 in the U.S.A. and Canada ($20.00 overseas, first class mail). Many bookstores also have *New Worlds* available to their customers. Ask for it.

Llewellyn's New Worlds of Mind and Spirit
P.O. Box 64383-830, St. Paul, MN 55164-0383, U.S.A.

TO ORDER BOOKS AND TAPES

If your book dealer does not have the books described, you may order them directly from the publisher by sending full price in U.S. funds, plus $3.00 for postage and handling for orders *under* $10.00; $4.00 for orders *over* $10.00. There are no postage and handling charges for orders over $50.00. Postage and handling rates are subject to change. We ship UPS whenever possible. Delivery guaranteed. Provide your street address as UPS does not deliver to P.O. Boxes. UPS to Canada requires a $50.00 minimum order. Allow 4-6 weeks for delivery. Orders outside the U.S.A. and Canada: Airmail—add retail price of book; add $5.00 for each non-book item (tapes, etc.); add $1.00 per item for surface mail. Mail orders to:

LLEWELLYN PUBLICATIONS
P.O. Box 64383-830, St. Paul, MN 55164-0383, U.S.A.

Prices subject to change without notice.

RUNE MAGIC
by Donald Tyson

Drawing upon historical records, poetic fragments, and the informed study of scholars, *Rune Magic* resurrects the ancient techniques of this tactile form of magic, and integrates those methods with modern occultism, so that anyone can use the runes in a personal magical system. For the first time, every known and conjectured meaning of all 33 known runes, including the 24 runes known as *futhark,* is available in one volume. In addition, *Rune Magic* covers the use of runes in divination, astral traveling, skrying, and on amulets and talismans. A complete rune ritual is also provided, and 24 rune words are outlined. Gods and Goddesses of the runes are discussed, with illustrations from the National Museum of Sweden.

0-87542-826-6, 210 pgs., 6 x 9, illus., softcover $9.95

THE NEW MAGUS
by Donald Tyson

The New Mangus serves as a personal system of magic. This book is filled with practical, usable magical techniques and rituals which anyone from any magical tradition can use. It includes instructions on how to design and perform rituals, create and use sigils, do invocations and evocations, do spiritual healings, learn rune magic, use god-forms, create telesmatic images, discover your personal guardian, create and use magical tools and muepts that have been put into terms, or *metaphors,* that are appropriate to life in our world today. That makes *The New Magus* the book on magic for today. If you have found that magic seems illogical, overcomplicated and not appropriate to your lifestyle, *The New Magus* is the book for you. It will change your ideas of magic forever!

0-87542-825-8, 6 x 9, illus., softcover $12.95

RITUAL MAGIC
by Donald Tyson

For thousands of years, men and women have practiced it despite the severe repression of sovereigns and priests. Now, *Ritual Magic* takes you into the heart of that entrancing, astonishing and at times mystifying secret garden of *magic*.

This book answers these and many other questions in a clear and direct manner. It explains what the occult revival is all about, reveals the foundations of practical ritual magic, showing how modern occultism grew from a single root into a number of clearly defined esoteric schools and pagan sects.

0-87542-835-5, 288 pgs., 6 x 9, ills., index, sftcvr. $12.95

THE MESSENGER
by Donald Tyson

Sealed inside a secret room of an old mansion in Nova Scotia is a cruel and uncontrollable entity, created years earlier by an evil magician. When the new owner of the mansion unknowingly releases the entity, it renews its malicious and murderous rampage.

Called on to investigate the strange phenomena are three women and four men—each with their own occult talents. As their investigation proceeds, the group members enter into a world of mystery and horror as they encounter astral battles, spirit possession—even death. In their efforts to battle the evil spirit, they use seance, hypnotic trance and magical rituals, the details of which are presented in fascinating and accurate detail.

Llewellyn Psi-Fi Fiction Series
0-87542-836-3, 240 pgs., mass market $4.99

THE GOLDEN DAWN
by Israel Regardie

Complete in one volume with further revision, expansion, and additional notes by Regardie, Cris Monnastre, and others. Also included are Initiation Ceremonies, important rituals for consecration and invocation, methods of meditation and magical working based on the Enochian Tablets, studies in the Tarot, and the system of Qabalistic Correspondences that unite the World's religions and magical traditions into a comprehensive and practical whole.

This volume is designed as a study and practice curriculum suited to both group and private practice. Meditation upon, and following with the Active Imagination, the Initiation Ceremonies are fully experiential without need of participation in group or lodge. A very complete reference encyclopedia of Western Magick.

0-87542-663-8, 840 pgs., 6 x 9, illus., sftcvr. $24.95

MODERN MAGICK
by Donald Michael Kraig

Modern Magick is the most comprehensive step-by-step introduction to the art of ceremonial magic ever offered. The eleven lessons will guide you from the easiest of rituals and the construction of your magickal tools through the highest forms of magick: designing your own rituals and doing pathworking. Along the way, you will learn the secrets of the Kabbalah in a clear and easy-to-understand manner. You will discover the true secrets of invocation (channeling) and evocation, and the missing information that will finally make the ancient grimoires, such as the "Keys of Solomon," comprehensible and usable. *Modern Magick* is designed so anyone can use it, and it is the perfect guidebook.

0-87542-324-8, 592 pgs., 6 x 9, illus., sftcvr. $17.95